Through Me to You

A Life Through Poetry, Stories, and Songs

Eve Wick

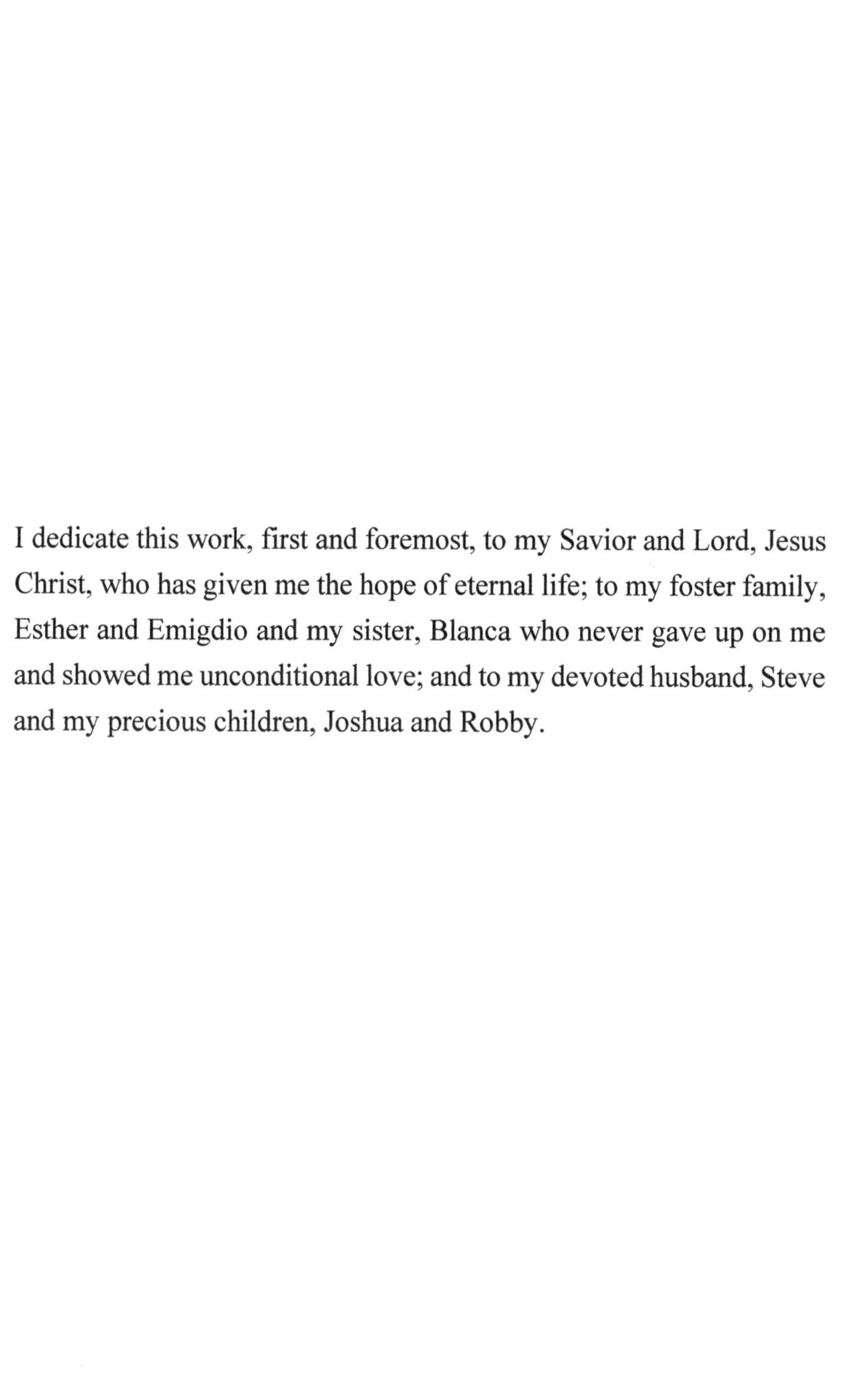

I dedicate this work, first and foremost, to my Savior and Lord, Jesus Christ, who has given me the hope of eternal life; to my foster family, Esther and Emigdio and my sister, Blanca who never gave up on me and showed me unconditional love; and to my devoted husband, Steve and my precious children, Joshua and Robby.

Contents

Preface

Through Me to You is a collection of my poems, stories, and songs from about the age of thirteen to the present time. It mirrors my growth as a writer and as a Christian. A verse of Scripture precedes each piece of writing in order to emphasize God's omnipresence. It is a testimony that no matter what we are going through, there is an answer in God's Word.

Most of my earlier works reflect an element of despair. Despair is a part of life that visits all of us. Sometimes, it stays longer than we would like. If we let despair stay, it will cripple us. These poems reveal the crippling effect despair had on my life and my worldview and the void it created.

Other writings show intense longing and the continual search for truth, which is ultimately found in Jesus. Some works reflect friendship and love, along with all of the emotions they stir up within us. Friendship and love, though worthy, were never meant to fill the void. Only one love brings purpose to life and completely fills the void: the love of Jesus.

Several of my poems express my deep love and identification with the African American soul. God has placed a burden on my heart for Africa, though I have never been to Africa and I am not African American. God works in mysterious ways. Amen!

Understanding and purpose are evident in my later pieces of writing. These writings tell about the love that changes us, the hope that takes residence in our hearts, and the assurance that answers our questions and lays aside all our searching.

The final part of the book contains songs. I am not a singer, musician, or songwriter, but God has placed these songs in my heart for a reason. Most of the songs don't have a tune—yet.

Only the love of God and the gift of Jesus can bring our lives full circle. I pray that these words will inspire you and encourage you to look to Christ, our only hope.

Hear my cry,

for I am very low.

Rescue me from my persecutors,

for they are too strong for me.

Bring me out of prison.

—Psalm 142:6–7 New Living Translation

Prisoner

Memories hold me prisoner
To the past.
The chains are heavy with
Thoughts iron-cast.
I long to be free,
To wing my way back home,
But I close the doors
That draw my friend near,
Wary to give Him a chance
To break those chains
And clear the guard,
Unlocking this cage of fear.

"See that you do not despise

one of these little ones.

For I tell you that their angels

in heaven always see the

face of my Father in heaven."

—Matthew 18:10-11 New International Version.

Child of the World

Profound wound,
New blood—
Tomorrow's child
Yesterday was

A seed
Transcended into flesh.
Nine months
Of motherly rest,

Safe and secure
Within the womb—
This creature knows
No other room.

Child of the world,
Born undefiled and blessed,
Men will show you
To be much less.

Jesus answered,

"Everyone who drinks this water

will be thirsty again,

but whoever drinks the water

I give them will never thirst.

Indeed, the water I give them

will become in them a spring of water

welling up to eternal life."

—John 4:13 – 14 NIV

Run. I Must Run.

Sweat, the sun at my back,
Trees in the distance,
The rustling of leaves.
Run. I must run.
Suddenly a voice:
"Where are you?"
"I do not know. I am lost." I reply.
"Where are you from?"
"Nowhere. I exist nowhere."
The voice continues,
"Where are you going?"
"Far, far away."

Sweat. The trees. Thirst.
Run. I must run.
In the distance, a brook
Sparkles,
Refreshing yet
Barely quenching me.
The voice returns:
"Who are you?"
Says the reflection,
"I do not know."
Run. I must run.

Where can I go from your spirit?
Or where can I flee from your presence?
—Psalm 139:7 New Revised Standard Version

Fantasy

Restless of sitting on stars
And staring out
At endless space,
My dry tears froze,
Withered into time …

Conversing with the void,
I could only hear
The silent weeping
Of the moon.
I yearned to hear
The voice of another.

Amid the confusion
And isolation,
You melted
My cold solitude
With a depth that
Penetrated dim
And clouded spaces
Within my soul.

In the mist,
I felt Your presence.
The fog ascended.
You threw light upon
My lonely existence.

You light a lamp for me.

The Lord, my God,

lights up my darkness.

—Psalm 18:28 NLT

The Night

Hand of darkness
That embraces life,
I am starved for your touch,
your hold so tight.

I ache to see you,
To know who you are,
Faceless companion,
Close yet so far.

I searched the day
While it was light.
The day grew black.
You are the night.

Would not God have discovered it,

since he knows the secrets of the heart?

—Psalm 44:21 NIV

Feeling

It is hidden.

It will always be there,

Hidden.

Many have searched for it,

But it has never been found.

I have searched for it too,

But it is too deep

For me

To rip it out of my soul.

It is the glory of God to conceal a matter;

to search out a matter is the glory of kings.

—Proverbs 25:2 NIV

Search Again

I am like the wind.

I go everywhere

And arrive no place.

I am in constant motion,

On a constant journey,

In a constant search

For the truth.

When the air is dry

And the leaves are still,

I have not gone.

I hide myself, waiting

To search again.

The Lord is close to the brokenhearted

and saves those who are crushed in spirit.

—Psalm 34:18 NIV

Empty

My insides are empty.

I feel nothing—

No pain, no pleasure.

I am numb

Of all feeling,

Of love.

But I say, love your enemies!

Pray for those who persecute you!

In that way, you will be acting as true

children of your Father in heaven.

—Matthew 5:44-45 NLT

I Unlove You Today

Time moves on;
The love has gone.

The heart deceives
What once I believed,

That love was found
And had me bound

To you, yesterday.

All night long on my bed

I looked for the one

my heart loves;

I looked for him

but did not find him.

—Song of Songs 3:1 NIV

Sweet Blindness

Sweet blindness,

So precious,

Yet I see.

Crippled emotion,

Untouched

In me.

Boundless

Its existence,

Experience young and old.

Faith in another being,

Hope,

Laughter of souls.

Prevails the unsearchable

Timeless affair.

I have but one question.

Song of heart

That plays within me:

Are you love or sensation?

Do not arouse or awaken

love until it so desires.

—Song of Songs 8:4 NIV

Heart from Heart

Every time I look at you,

I ask you to be mine.

Yet silent eyes, however true,

Can show no signs.

If only my eyes could converse,

They would tell you all,

Hold you captive with one verse,

And break this wall,

That divides the two

And tears apart

Me from you,

Heart from heart.

Wait for the Lord; be strong
and take heart and wait for the Lord.

—Psalm 27:14 NIV

Two Paths

Two paths meet along the way.

A part of the plan?

A moment? A day?

Are we to judge

Where we have no say?

Let it ride.

Move on.

Just pray.

Not only so, but we also glory in our sufferings,

because we know that suffering produces

perseverance; perseverance, character;

and character, hope.

—Romans 5:3–4 NIV

The Irony of Life

I would rather live a good deal of my life in

Suffering so that when I am finally given

Joy, I will recognize it as such, appreciate it,

And be able to distinguish between joy and

Sorrow, than to have always lived a life of

Bliss and never been given the opportunity

To know the value of each, to differentiate

Between the two.

Even if my father and mother abandon me,

the Lord will hold me close.

—Psalm 27:10 NLT

Poem from a Foster Child

Mother's dead now,
Father remains unknown.
I only knew foster parents,
Yet with them, I felt at home.

Then we were separated
By time and too many miles.
When we finally reunited,
I was no longer a child.

The years had gone by,
Causing us both to change
And leaving me questioning why
Our lives were so poorly arranged.

How good and pleasant it is when

God's people live together in unity!

—Psalm 133:1 NIV

A World

From time to time, I imagine a world
With its nations at peace,
Joined by friendship and love;
A world where people accept each other
As they are, not by what they have; a
World where the people are not judged
But, indeed, united—a world that does
Not exist.

Turn to me and be gracious to me,

for I am lonely and afflicted.

—Psalm 25:16 NIV

Loner

Loner,
Cold world.

A sunny day
With colors
And flowers
And love

Turned a loner
Into a somebody
And a cold world
Into a nice place
To be.

I applied my heart to what I observed

and learned a lesson from what I saw.

—Proverbs 24:32 NIV

To Suffer

No one has gone through life
And never had to suffer.
The farther one walks,
The more the road has to offer.
Experience is life's best teacher—
This we cannot deny—
and time the best healer
To mend the hurt deep inside.
So if we must learn to suffer, in return,
We learn to appreciate
Life's little lessons
And our own fates.

Jesus replied, "Very truly I tell you, no one can see the kingdom of God unless they are born again."

– John 3:3 NIV

Be

No longer to believe in yourself

Is a reflection.

Never accept, but question,

He who believes.

No longer to love yourself

Is defeat.

Overcome, internally seek,

He who is.

No longer to seek the truth

Is death.

Reborn, lest regret.

Be.

"Come to me, all who are weary and heavy-laden,
and I will give you rest. Take My yoke upon you and
learn from Me, for I am gentle and humble
in heart, and you will find rest for your souls."
—Matthew 11:28–29 New American Standard Bible

His Touch

I was lost and weary.

Then one day,

A kind man stopped

And wiped away my sweat.

And I cried

As I never had before.

When He picked me up

From the ground

And our eyes met,

For the first time I saw

That He was Jesus,

And I no longer had to search

For He held me tightly,

And His touch was warm.

Then, all of a sudden,

It no longer hurt,

And I was happy in His embrace,

For there I slept

And felt, indeed, I belonged.

And we know that God causes

all things to work together for

good to those who love God,

to those who are called

according to His purpose.

—Romans 8:28 NASB

Why?

(For Sonja)

Why?

For what reason?

For whose benefit?

For what gain?

To what end?

For what purpose?

Why can't I make sense

Out of senselessness?

I need questions answered.

I want explanations.

Don't I deserve an answer?

God, I am angry!

Why?

My child, all things work for

Good for those who love the Lord.

Some answers come in time,

In a moment, in a realization.

Some questions will never be answered

here and are reserved for heaven's doors.

But know that every question will

Ultimately be answered

And therein lies our hope.

Each of you should use whatever

gift you have received to serve others,

as faithful stewards of God's grace

in its various forms.

—1 Peter 4:10 NIV

Poem from a Gifted Child

I have a gift
I cannot hide,
One that only opens
From inside.

I never asked
For such a gift.
Please, understand
My simple wish.

Don't unwrap it
Unless you first ask.
Don't toy with it;
It just won't last.

Just enjoy it
And hold it tight.
Don't reject it;
Know my plight.

Each one of us has a gift,
Different and diverse.
Help mine to be a blessing
And not a curse!

Hatred stirs up conflict,

but love covers over all wrongs.

—Proverbs 10:12 NIV

Rain Acceptance

I wish the beauty

Of each person

Would blind us

From hatred,

That all our colors

Could be splashed

Across the sky

And rain acceptance

From

Above.

God saw everything that he had made,

and indeed, it was very good.

—Genesis 1:31 NRSV

You Don't Own Your Color

You don't own your color.

God loans it to you, and

When you die,

It returns to the earth.

We are all part

Of God's landscape.

As every painter

Decides what he needs

For his canvas

And where the colors need to be,

God has painted us all perfectly.

They will know that I am the Lord, when

I break the bars of their yoke and rescue them

from the hands of those who enslaved them.

—Ezekiel 34:27 NIV

Torn From My Arms

Torn from my arms,

I hear my babies cry.

Lord, lead me on;

My soul yearns to die.

My eyes gaze upon this man,

The very heart of me,

As he is led away,

They ignore my plea.

I throw myself to the ground,

My family torn apart.

Amid the cries and moans,

I hear the bidding start.

The Lord said, "What have you done? Listen!
Your brother's blood cries out to me from the ground."

—Genesis 4:10 NIV

Break My Bones

Break my bones,
Shatter my knees,
But you will never kill
The Africa in me.

The blood you shed
This day will seep
Into the ground,
And you will reap,
From your own hands,
An Africa planted
In a new land.

It was for freedom that Christ set us free;

therefore keep standing firm and do not

be subject again to a yoke of slavery.

—Galatians 5:1 NASB

Chains Of Agony

Chains of agony
That bind my tiny hands;
Chains of misery
That take me from my homeland.

Confused and dazed,
I am pushed aboard
This floating city
Traveling abroad.

Africa, O Africa,
My spirit never leaves.
Sweet freedom, O freedom,
Sweep gently over me.

Praise be to the Lord, to God our Savior,

who daily bears our burdens.

—Psalm 68:19 NIV

I'm Going to Hide Behind the Mountain

Hide me from my

Godless enemies.

Daylight seems farther

Than eternity.

Wrapped in the still

Of the dark night,

I view those

Precious in my sight.

But such a view

Is only imagined,

Perceived.

Over the loss of

My fellow travelers,

I grieve.

I cry out in

Anguish and fear,

Yet I know the

Lord is near.

May the groans of the prisoners come before you;

with your strong arm preserve those condemned to die.

—Psalm 79:11 NIV

Way Too Soon

Brother, I'm gonna catch my train.
Gonna take me to victory.
Brother, I'm gonna break those chains
That tie me to slavery.

Brother, listen carefully
To that sweet, sweet melody.
Soon this plantation
Will be a faint memory.

But my ride ended way too soon,
And my dreams were shattered like my bones.
All my hopes disappeared
As the air was filled
With my screams and moans.

For now we see in a mirror
dimly, but then face to face;
now I know in part, but then
I will know fully just as I also
have been fully known.
—1 Corinthians 13:12 NASB

Baggage Claim

The pain we feel inside our bag of skin is so unique. I may feel strands of your pain, but only you know the depths of what you feel. But know that if you can find the courage to rely on God's strength instead of your own, then you have matured. Overwhelmed by problems, the last thing we want to lose is our false sense of security; however, if we simply let go and let God do His work in us, we will be truly secure.

We all have problems. I cannot own your problems, and certainly you cannot own mine for as much as we try. So travel light through life. Know your baggage and claim it. Sometimes, in our most intimate relationships, our vision is clouded, and we cannot distinguish ownership. It is then we must understand that the individual who stands to lose the most is the true owner. Pure knowledge cannot help us here; wisdom will show us our needs. Then love can truly take place—the love of oneself, the love of another.

In times of crisis, only the true owner of a problem can solve it. The Holy Spirit will lead you. Your friends can listen and be a mirror that cares, for they will never use power over you. In times of crisis, when you are blamed, judged, threatened, and lectured, then you are a victim of power. Only Christ can make individuals truly even.

We all have a window we look out of, and in that window we see our own view. That's costly to accept at times but even more costly would be to shut that window!

Live holy lives before me because I, God,
am holy. I have distinguished you
from the nations to be my very own.
—Leviticus 20:26 (The Message)

The Day the Lady Cried

Each day, I stand by the harbor's side,
A staunch reminder of American pride.
But today my skin of metal wept,
My hands trembled, and my heart leapt
When the land shuddered and my people died.

Standing alone, helpless, I saw
Senseless, evil acts of war.
The skyline turned dim and gray.
Implosions tore foundations away.

Thousands of innocent Americans died
When jetliners were forced to collide,
Crumbling sister towers onto city streets,
As hundreds looked on in disbelief.

If metal and stone could move,
I would have saved the towers from ruin.
But I had to stand at my post.
That day, Americans needed liberty the most.

Your sun will never set;

Your moon will not go down.

For the Lord will be your everlasting light.

Your days of mourning will come to an end.

—Isaiah 60:20 NLT

Perfection

A man lived alone, and in his loneliness he strived for perfection. He had not always lived this way; he once was like you or me. He had felt pain and joy, and he had cried, rejoiced, shared and sacrificed. Yet one day, he questioned himself and his actions. He saw no true reason for being and isolated himself from others.

Till this day, he lives in isolation, and in his isolation he seeks truth. The only light that enters the room comes from a single window. There he contemplates and views the parched, dry grass that extends to the forest up ahead.

One day, the sun ceased to shine, and the man was covered by darkness. The darkness was ugly and threatened the man. He could not find perfection, only his own ignorance. The truth revealed itself to him, and he was embittered. His life was over, yet he had never lived; time passed, and he became one with the darkness.

Behold, You desire truth in the

innermost being, and in the hidden part

You will make me know wisdom.

—Psalm 51:6 NASB

The Question

Countless years ago, a young child asked of his father, "What is wisdom?"

The father, preoccupied with other things, hastily told his son, "Why do you ask such foolish questions?" And the father turned around and walked away.

The child, feeling rejected, approached his mother. "Mom, what is wisdom?"

She looked at her son and said, "That is what you learn in school."

Not feeling satisfied with that answer, he asked his grandfather the same question. The grandfather, patiently and in his quiet way, replied, "That is part of a good education."

Kissing his grandfather, the boy walked out of his house and went on his way to school. Upon arriving there, he approached his teacher and asked again, "What is wisdom?"

Dismissing the little boy's inquiry, the teacher responded, "You're much too young to be asking such things."

For the rest of the day, the boy sat in class and said nothing. He walked back home at the end of the day. As the boy wandered down the dirt road, lost in thought, he felt the irregular shapes of the stones under his feet and smelled the fragrance of the blooming flowers all around him. It began to drizzle, and he could feel the raindrops on his skin and savored their taste. As he beheld the extraordinary beauty of this ordinary path, he heard the fluttering of winged creatures up above. And as the boy gazed upon the wondrous sky, he knew he need not ask that question again.

Who among you is wise and understanding?

Let him show by his good behavior

his deeds in the gentleness of wisdom.

—James 3:13 NASB

The Guest

Many years ago, our guest bathroom became a refuge for an unlikely guest. My father silently welcomed this tiny visitor into our home. Wounded, this frail creature needed care. My father, a man of great stature and character, swaddled its broken body with his loving hands. Clutching it close to his chest, Dad led this frightened creature into a small bathroom. I followed close behind as the early-summer breeze escorted us into our makeshift infirmary. The symphonic flow of running water composed our startled guest, as my father prepared a bottle in its honor.

Slowly, my father fed this gentle baby as the mirror captured a tender tear running down my father's face. In my mind's eye, I recorded this instant in time knowing that it would last longer than any photograph, for this memory would never fade. As each drop of nourishment entered the creature's body, a warm, cozy feeling entered mine. The easiness my heart felt could only be matched by the simplicity of that moment.

Surveying that scene, those many years ago, my father seemed larger than life; a foundation upon a foundation. His compassion, more enduring than the walls that surrounded him that day, is a frequent guest in my heart each time I visit him in my memories. The mercy he showed that afternoon to one of God's smallest creatures was, indeed, a noble act. For you see, this baby was a wounded fledgling and its bottle was an eyedropper full of love.

Therefore go and make disciples of all nations,

baptizing them in the name of the Father

and of the Son and of the Holy Spirit.

—Matthew 28:19 NIV

Gospel Angels

Gospel angels, each one a child of tender faith—
Messengers not made of tinsel, wood, or clay
But carved by the Creator in His loving way,
that jewels pale in comparison to such display.

(Chorus)
The gospel cries out to be shared.
The pages weep until they tear.
And then the Word of God floats
Through the air,
Hoping that an angel will be there.

Each Christian, unlike a diamond in the rough,
Is a courier molded for one sole reason.
Others may not see this rare jewel enough,
So the gospel must transcend time and season.

(Chorus)
As imperfect as we may be,
Only our lips can spread the Word.
Yes, God has chosen you and me.
Brother, sister, haven't you heard?

(Chorus)
Will you be there? Will you be there?
Will you be an angel, an angel that cares?
Will you be there? Will you be there?
Will you be an angel, an angel that cares?

I in them and you in me—

so that they may be brought to complete unity.

—John 17:23 NIV

Just Shine

I cannot find my life in a color.

I cannot find this life of mine.

If all I see are shades of others,

I'll never find this life of mine.

I cannot find my life in a color.

I'll never find this life of mine.

Know your culture, know your brother;

Then you will find a whole lifetime.

(Chorus)

Know your culture, share your color;

Then you'll know how to love others.

Know your culture, share your color;

Then you'll know how to love others.

So I will find my life in my culture.

Then colors will not confuse my mind.

Culture has no tones or colors

That cannot be shared, just shine.

(Chorus)

Just shine!

For this command is a lamp, this teaching is a light,
and correction and instruction are the way to life.

—Proverbs 6:23 NIV

Ode to Mary

Your life's an open book of love,
Pages once sewn with words of trust—
Born free yet still somehow enslaved
By ignorance and painful words of hate.

(Chorus)
Mary McCloud Bethune,
Can you teach us
To be like you?
Mary McCloud Bethune,
Can you teach us
To be just like you?

Refuge came in the form of words,
Pages simply not meant for her.
Somehow her dream would never die.
Mary read, fueled by ancient pride.

(Chorus)

Chosen to be the one to learn,
An honor Mary deserved and earned.
Teacher and advocate of rights,
Others would keep her dream in sight.

(Chorus)

Beloved, do not be surprised at the fiery ordeal
that is taking place among you to test you, as
though something strange were happening to
you. But rejoice insofar as you are sharing
Christ's sufferings, so that you may also be glad
and shout for joy when his glory is revealed.

—1 Peter 4:12-13 NRSV

Praise Your Way through the Darkness

(Chorus)
Praise your way through the darkness
When all seems bleak and dim,
For when we truly suffer,
The light shines brighter then.

We cannot see the light
When we are steeped in pain,
But if you can appreciate the darkness,
Your life will never be the same.

For surely the road is long
With little light up ahead,
But experience can teach us
We are still being led.

(Chorus)

The darkness somehow turns out
To be an unlikely friend,
As it shrouds the hurt and pain
Until we finally mend.

So when we come out into the light,
Our lives are forever changed,
Not just because we can see clearer
But because of the joy we reclaim.

So that with one mind and one voice

you may glorify the God and

Father of our Lord Jesus Christ.

—Romans 15:6 NIV

We Are One

(Chorus)
We are one
For He has won
The battle for our souls.

We can stand together
Because He stood alone
And hung on the cross
Amid the cries and moans.

Together we can stand
For He made his love known,
And He asks in return
To let His love be shown.

(Chorus)

One is not a desolate number
When that number means all,
For the Lord won the world's battle
When Jesus answered God's call.

He won the battle for all
Who truly would believe.
The victory is for one
And all who humbly receive.

(Chorus)

Stand together;
Don't stand alone.
Make his presence
Forever known.

"Now then, listen, you lover of pleasure,

lounging in your security and saying to yourself,

'I am, and there is none besides me.

—Isaiah 47:8 NIV

Too Cool for Calvary

Wiping the sleep from my eyes,
I refuse to wake up,
Knowing that my day runneth over,
But I drink not from Your cup.

For my cup is black,
And its taste is strong,
But not the kind of strength
For which I long.

(Chorus)
Lord, have I become
Too cool for Calvary?
Becoming more and more
Like the world surrounding me?

My only reflection comes
From the mirror each morn,
And it fails to sustain me
From dawn to dawn.

I know that the reflection I need
Comes only from Your Word,
But my schedule is too booked
For You to be heard.

(Chorus)

Carefully choosing the clothes
That I will wear for display
Makes me a slave of fashion,
Not a servant of Your way.

Rushing off to work,
Still not saying Your name,
I brush my hair from my face
Without a bit of shame.

(Chorus)

Behind the wheel I hear
The familiar Christian tunes,
My mind focused on the beat,
The meaning lost too soon.

"If you belonged to the world, it would love you as its own. As
it is, you do not belong to the world but I have chosen
you out of the world." [John 15:19 NIV].

(Chorus)

The meaning lost too soon.
Brother, can't you hear that tune?
The meaning lost too soon.
Sister, can't you hear that tune?

His master replied, "Well done,

good and faithful servant!"

Matthew 25:21 NIV

A Faithful Servant of God

A faithful servant of God,
Obedient and true,
Our sweet Patricia touched
Many lives not few.

Born in Middletown, New York,
Of parents Gillen and Roberson,
A dedicated daughter
And a sister like no one.

(Chorus)
The Lord must take
His dear ones,
So the angels can sing.
Heaven's clouds part open,
So she can take wing.

An extraordinary student
Produced a fine nurse indeed.
She served her community
And so many in need.

(Chorus)

And a mother to many,
All her children and countless friends.
She's our true mother,
And that will never end.

(Chorus)

Her earthly mission completed
Early that Sunday morn.
We still cannot believe
Our Patricia is gone.

"Her life ended way too soon,"
Our selfish motives would surely chime.
But now she can finally rest,
Sweet mother of mine.

(Chorus)

Afterword

I had the opportunity to write this book while I was at home recovering from an emergency surgery. For six months, I endured incessant pain caused by nerve damage. The chronic pain diminished my will to live, but I knew that God had saved my life for a reason. This trial allowed me to hear clearly from Him. Although, I had created this book idea fourteen years ago, now was the time to gather this collection of writings and Scripture verses for publication. God's timing is always perfect!

Due to the nerve damage, I was unable to sit and type the manuscript so I wish to thank my son, Robby, who typed the entire manuscript and helped me with numerous revisions. My son and I became very close which was truly a gift from God. Additionally, I want to thank my youngest son, Joshua, who encouraged me daily with his kind words and delectable hugs and to my husband, who supported me throughout the process.

I pray that you will turn your trials into opportunities. You, also, have the opportunity right now to accept Jesus as your Savior. If you wish to make Jesus Christ the Lord of your life, you can say a simple prayer like the one below. Salvation is not about joining a religion, but it is about entering into a relationship with Jesus.

Dear Jesus, I know that I am not perfect. I ask You to forgive my sins. I open the door of my heart to You. I acknowledge that You died on the cross for my sins and that You are alive today. I receive You as my Lord and Savior. I am trusting in You to give me eternal life. Thank You for saving me. Amen.

Printed by Libri Plureos GmbH in Hamburg, Germany